Especially for: _____

From: _____

_____

purr-ables from heaven

M.R. Wells, Connie Fleishauer, and Dottie P. Adams

rachaelhale

HARVEST HOUSE PUBLISHERS

EUGENE, OREGON

Purr-ables from Heaven—*Gift Edition*

© Dissero Brands Limited (New Zealand) 2008.
All worldwide rights reserved.
www.rachaelhale.com

Text Copyright © 2006 by M.R. Wells, Connie Fleishauer, and Dottie P. Adams

Published by Harvest House Publishers
Eugene, Oregon 97402
www.harvesthousepublishers.com

ISBN-13: 978-0-7369-2204-3
ISBN-10: 0-7369-2204-0

Design and production by Garborg Design Works, Savage, Minnesota

Harvest House Publishers has made every effort to trace the ownership of all poems and quotes. In the event of a question arising from the use of a poem or quote, we regret any error made and will be pleased to make the necessary correction in future editions of this book.

Scripture quotations are taken from the HOLY BIBLE, NEW INTERNATIONAL VERSION®. NIV®. Copyright©1973, 1978, 1984 by the International Bible Society. Used by permission of Zondervan. All rights reserved.

Printed in China

08 09 10 11 12 13 14 15 / LP / 10 9 8 7 6 5 4 3 2

kitty adulation

Introductory Paws

The ancient Egyptians got it all wrong. They revered, even worshipped, cats. God wasn't too pleased, but we doubt the cats minded. They probably lapped up all the adulation they were given. They're still doing so today.

Actually, we humans were born to have dominion over all other creatures and worship the Creator we share. But our kitties don't always get that straight, and neither do we. Perhaps that's what makes them such a marvelous mirror to reflect our own foibles and God's care and love for us in spite of them.

We are grateful to our kitties for giving us a glimpse of ourselves from God's perspective, and a window into His great love for us and patience with us. We pray our stories may spur you to delight in the Lord and curl up in His lap.

the treat not taken

Taste All of God's Goodness

I set out the yummy new delicacy beside the kitties' normal meal. Which would they take, prime choice select grilled steak or sale-priced cat food? I wanted to treat them to something special. I was also curious to see if they would sample a food they had never tasted before.

Sammy, one of the neighbor cats, was standing by the food bowl when I brought out the steak. She looked at the steak and kept right on eating the cat food. Then our cat Michelin came

God's gifts put man's best dreams to shame.

Elizabeth Barrett Browning

around. She also looked at the beef and walked away. I had to guess they just assumed it wouldn't be good and decided to ignore it.

Finally our cat Milkshake appeared. He eyed the meat. He looked at the other two felines. He saw that they didn't want it, so he gobbled it up. He wasn't afraid to try something new, so he had a wonderful treat.

Watching those cats refuse a gift they didn't understand reminded me of how we often miss out on God's gifts because they are unfamiliar and we don't realize how they can bless us. When God offers treats, we can trust that they are wonderful.

I had to guess they just assumed it wouldn't be good and decided to ignore it.

wally on our shoulders
Curl Up on God's Lap

Wally was our tiniest kitten, but she gave us many big lessons. She ran the whole family for a while, small as she was. Whenever any of us would come home, the first thing we would do is look for her. We wanted to hold her—but we also didn't want to step on her.

When we were sitting in the living room, Wally usually perched on someone's lap, or better yet, their shoulders. My husband Steve's broad shoulders were a favorite spot. She would roll into a little ball and fall asleep far above her world. She didn't seem at all afraid to be up there. In fact, this was where she seemed to feel most comfortable and safe.

We are God's children. We can rest on His shoulders, just as Wally did on Steve's.

The eternal God is your refuge, and underneath are the everlasting arms.
DEUTERONOMY 33:27

9

jumping from the helmet

Caring Builds Trust

You cannot do a kindness too soon, for you never know how soon it will be too late.

RALPH WALDO EMERSON

Sid's kittens were fluffy with gray-and-white stripes, and they lived in a motorcycle helmet. Usually our mother cats found a soft place to keep their kittens while they were small, but Sid used a helmet on the garage floor. It was large, with thick black padding inside.

One day Sid met with an accident and her orphaned kittens were too young to care for themselves. So our three children came to the rescue. Christy, John, and Karen each got a special bottle ready. Then they slowly and quietly crept into the garage, calling the kittens

11

by name. In just seconds, they heard little meows coming from the helmet. They coaxed the kitties out and each child fed one.

The first few times, the kittens were reluctant to leave the safety of their helmet, but before long they were jumping from it to greet their human friends. It was quite a picture to see the little ones as they leaped from the helmet one by one and walked in a straight line toward the children.

There are many people who, like those kittens, hesitate to jump from their helmet. They are not sure others love them and want to meet their needs. But like those kitties, they will often respond if someone takes the time to care about them.

There are many people who, like those kittens, hesitate to jump from their helmet.

picture purr-fect

Look at Life from God's Perspective

Rajah was a picture purr-fect kitten. She was beautiful and appeared to pose every time she saw a camera. My favorite photo is of Rajah perched up on a fishbowl. She would sit there for hours watching the fish swim around. From her seat up above, she could see everything going on in the water.

I'm sure the fish were not at all happy about Rajah's antics. If they could have understood their plight, they probably would have felt trapped.

I'm not just a fish swimming in circles. I'm God's child, and I can watch from the top with Him. Rather than let the world cloud my vision, I can ask God to focus the eyes of my heart—so I can see clearly. Not trapped, but triumphant!

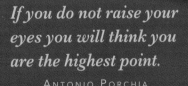

If you do not raise your eyes you will think you are the highest point.

Antonio Porchia

15

It is amazing what you can accomplish if you do not care who gets the credit.

the licked-up glory
Seek God's Glory, Not Yours

When Kitty lived mainly in the house, she found ways to entertain herself that made her happy and content. One day she played with a fly on the living room window. Although the fly didn't appear to be having any fun, Kitty batted at it first with one paw and then the other. She tried to bite it. She even licked it a little. Finally she pinned it to the window with her paw—only to release it again.

Kitty seemed rather proud of her work, but I doubt the poor fly could have flown away in the end. It never got the chance. While Kitty continued

to swipe at it, Max, our Boston Terrier, sat patiently watching. All at once he dashed to the window and licked up the fly with one swipe of his tongue. Then he strolled away while Kitty just sat there, astounded. In a flash, all she'd worked for was licked up by someone else.

I always felt Kitty walked away from that fly feeling cheated. Sometimes we feel that we do all the work and others walk away with all the glory. But if we remember that everything we do is for the glory of God, it really doesn't matter if someone else licks it all up.

Kitty just sat there, astounded. In a flash, all she'd worked for was licked up by someone else.

moving day

When Life Changes, God Doesn't

Change is not made without inconvenience, even from worse to better.

RICHARD HOOKER

There he was, sleeping contentedly on my belly. I had just awakened from a short nap on the sofa on this cold, rainy day. As I stirred, he opened his eyes and blinked them in happy recognition. *My, how far this kitty has come,* I thought. *He is starting to feel at home.*

Mooch had recently come to us from another family. This change had been thrust upon him when his owner passed away. Everything was different from what he had known in his previous four years.

I've heard it said that the one constant thing in life is change. In one brief moment something can shift and life becomes radically different. This was true for Mooch. And this is true for us. Though everything else can change in a moment, God is the same, always and forever—and we can always count on Him.

a cat in doll's clothing

Be Who God Made You

The notion to play dress-up with my cat was probably inspired by Mom. She loved pictures of kitties decked out in human clothing. But when I put my doll's dress on Fluffy, my pet was less than amused. The little dress just wasn't made for an animal that runs on all fours. It hog-tied that cat. After snapping a picture of my miserable feline looking less than pleased in her new attire, I mercifully released her from her cloth prison.

I'm sure if Fluffy knew human speech, she would have given me a

Always be a first-rate version of yourself, instead of a second-rate version of somebody else.

JUDY GARLAND

23

talking-to. She would have said, "Silly human, what were you thinking? I'm not some two-dimensional greeting card or postcard kitty. I'm a real cat. And real cats don't wear puffed sleeves!"

Looking back, I can smile at my efforts to stuff Fluffy into that ill-fitting garment. But I've realized I've done the same thing to myself. I've tried to stuff myself into other people's personalities or talents, and they haven't fit me any better than that dress fit Fluffy.

I no longer wish to scrunch myself into a doll's dress. I want to revel in the one-of-a-kind person God made me to be, and model His creation for His glory forever.

"I'm a real cat. And real cats don't wear puffed sleeves!"

Evenings are a time when cats congregate in our backyard. They curl up on the porch, snoozing comfortably and feeling safe—till Stuart starts playing his favorite game. Stuart is our dog. He loves chasing cats. He dives at them, and they flee in terror, leaping over the back fence to safety—all except Milkshake.

Milkshake refuses to run in terror. After Stuart clears the yard of the other felines, he and Milkshake sniff each other. They seem to have reached an understanding. Milkshake has faced his fears and refuses to be chased from his yard—and Stuart has accepted that.

Just as Milkshake has taken a stand, we can stand our ground against those who would chase us out of anyplace we know we have the right to be.

chasing fears
Stand Firm in Your Faith

Courage is contagious. When a brave man takes a stand, the spines of others are stiffened.
BILLY GRAHAM

I have lived, Sir, a long time, and the longer I live, the more convincing proofs I see of this truth—that God governs in the affairs of men.

BENJAMIN FRANKLIN

cat-astrophic salad
God Is Bigger than Our Bloopers

Today was the day. I'd finally found a special recipe for the church cook-off—a salmon salad with fruit. I put it in a lovely china bowl and covered it carefully.

My nephew Mark carried the dish to the car and was told to guard it with his life. Just as I was about to go outside, Mark came in and handed me the empty bowl. He had set it on top of the car for a moment, and Kitty had knocked it into the dirt.

I was determined not to let a cat-induced catastrophe ruin things.

29

We rushed outside and scooped up whatever parts of the salad hadn't touched the dirt or been licked by my cat. We put what we'd salvaged in half a cantaloupe shell, added a little greenery, and it actually looked pretty good.

We had a great time at the church dinner. Nobody knew what had happened to the salad. And it won first prize!

I am grateful that God is bigger than my mistakes. It comforts me to know that when I, in my humanness, knock the gorgeous salmon salad of His perfect will into the dirt, He can scoop up the pieces, rearrange them, and use them for His glory.

There are few things in life more heart-warming than to be welcomed by a cat.

TAY HOHOFF